· MEET ·
OSMAN HAMDI

Read With You Center for
Excellence in STEAM Education

Read With You

Text & illustration copyright © 2022 Read With You
All rights reserved. No part of this book may be reproduced, stored in a retrieval system, or transmitted in any form or by any means, electronic, mechanical, photocopying, recording, or otherwise, without express written permission of the publisher.
Published by Read With You Publishing. Printed in the United States of America.
Read With You and associated logos are trademarks and/or registered trademarks of Read With You L.L.C.
ISBN: 979-8-88618-098-5
First Edition January 2022

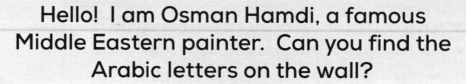

The Scholar, 1878

Lady of Constantinople, 1881

Persian Carpet Dealer on the Street, 1888

Portrait of Naile Hanim, undated

Two Musician Girls, 1880

The Public Scribe, 1910

The Tortoise Trainer, 1906

Man Reading the Quran, 1910

Find Examples

This painting is titled *Quranic Instruction* (1890). It shows the details of many kinds of Eastern architecture.

What do you see in the building that is unlike buildings you have been in?

What colors do you see the most? Would you paint your house these colors?

Describe the clothing the men are wearing. What would it feel like to wear these clothes?

Connect

This painting is *Young Woman Reading* (1880). At a time when many women did not read, Osman Hamdi celebrated smart women.

How are her clothes different from the clothes that men wear in Osman Hamdi's paintings?

Can you find another window in the book with a similar design?

How is this room different from rooms in your own home? How is it similar?

Craft

Option 1

1. Find a pattern you like. The pattern can be from your clothes, a piece of furniture, or a decoration.

2. Draw a picture of the pattern. Change some of the colors or shapes to make it unique.

Option 2

1. Look at the picture of the tortoise trainer. Many people think this painting shows how hard it is to teach people new skills. Choose an animal that represents how you learn.

2. Draw a picture of that animal learning something.

Made in United States
North Haven, CT
17 May 2023

36678440R00022